AF086454

Muscat
Our City, Our Home

Written by
Stephen Rickard

Ransom

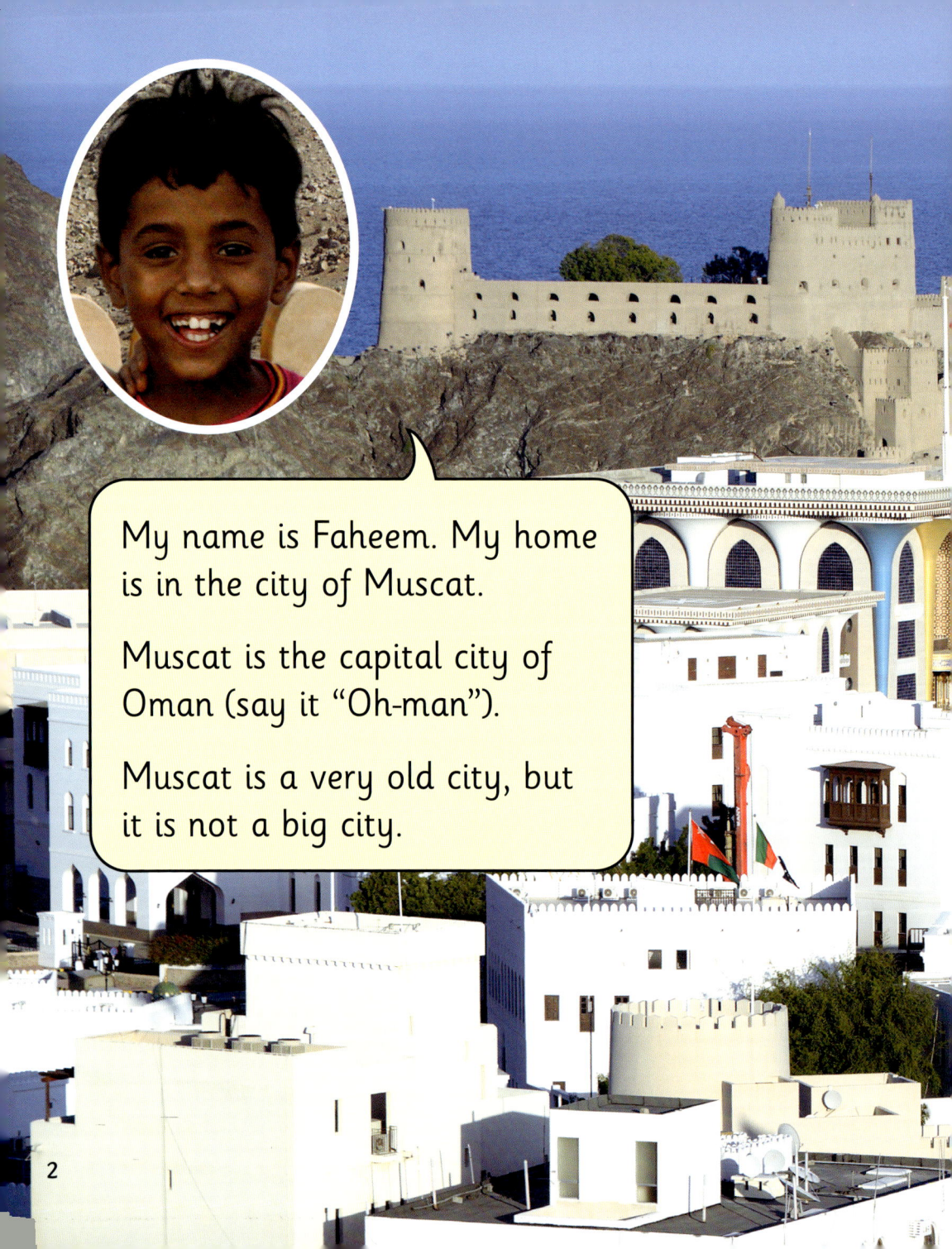

My name is Faheem. My home is in the city of Muscat.

Muscat is the capital city of Oman (say it "Oh-man").

Muscat is a very old city, but it is not a big city.

Would you like to visit Muscat?

Well, you can read this book and judge for yourself!

The sea next to Muscat is deep, so big ships can dock here. Muscat has always been an important port.

This is the old part of the city. This is where people like to stretch out in the sun and watch the boats.

It all makes a fantastic picture!

> Behind Muscat you can see the mountains. They are called the Al Hajar mountains. They are high and rocky.
>
> They are a perfect place to have adventures!

If you stand on a mountain ridge, you can see for a long way.

In Muscat it is never cold.

In winter-time it is sunny and dry. In the summer it is always very hot and very dry. The temperature can be up to 45 degrees.

We never see much moisture in the summer-time!

In the summer it is often too hot to stay outside.

So people go outside at the beginning of the day and at the end of the day.

When it is hottest, people stay inside, away from the hot sun.

We are an Arab people and we speak Arabic.

We are Muslims too.

Islam is very important. It teaches us to be good people.

But you will find lots of different people in Muscat.

People from many different parts of the world come to Muscat to work.

So we get a huge mixture of people!

We like to go shopping.

There are some big, modern shops in Muscat.

We like to go to the markets. In the markets the shops are not so big. There is a good mixture too, with lots of different kinds of shops.

Some shops can mend things too.

Don't forget to bring some money with you!

If you like nature, you can see lots of different wild creatures just outside the city.

Sometimes you can see vultures.

If you are lucky, you can even see dolphins!

Dolphins

Muscat is a fantastic place to stay.

Would you like to come and visit us?

Then you could see our city with your own eyes and judge for yourself!